Twenty-Thousand Leagues Under the Sea

Jules Verne

TEACHER GUIDE

NOTE:

The trade book edition of the novel used to prepare this guide is found in the Novel Units catalog and on the Novel Units website. Using other editions may have varied page references.

Please note: We have assigned Interest Levels based on our knowledge of the themes and ideas of the books included in the Novel Units sets, however, please assess the appropriateness of this novel or trade book for the age level and maturity of your students prior to reading with them. You know your students best!

BN 978-1-58130-849-5

To order, contact your local school supply store, or:

Toll-Free Fax: 877.716.7272
Phone: 888.650.4224
3901 Union Blvd., Suite 155
St. Louis, MO 63115

sales@novelunits.com

novelunits.com

Table of Contents

Skills and Strategies

Thinking
Analysis, compare/contrast, brainstorm, critical thinking, sequence

Vocabulary
Target words, definitions

Literary Elements
Characterization, simile, metaphor, plot development, setting, theme, irony, allusion, genre, universality

Writing
Poetry, characterization, essay, epilogue

Listening/Speaking
Discussion, oral report, film viewing

Comprehension
Cause/effect, prediction

Across the Curriculum
Music—appropriate background music; Art—montage, sketch, model; Current Events—newspaper and magazine articles; Geography—map

Genre: fiction—adventure

Setting: oceans and seas of the world; 1866–1867

Point of View: first person

Themes: adventure, survival, loyalty, friendship, vengeance

Conflict: person vs. person; person vs. nature; person vs. self; person vs. society

Plot: After becoming captives of Captain Nemo aboard the *Nautilus*, Professor Aronnax and his companions explore marine life while plotting to escape.

Style: narrative

Tone: adventurous, contemplative

Date of First Publication: 1870

Summary

Professor Aronnax, accompanied by his faithful servant Conseil, embarks on a hazardous mission to rid the seas of a huge monster. After being swept overboard, the two men and Ned Land, a harpooner, are imprisoned aboard a submarine, the *Nautilus*, by Captain Nemo, a genius driven by bitterness and revenge. The three captives encounter incredible adventures during their voyage aboard Nemo's amazing vessel under the world's oceans and seas.

Characters

Professor Aronnax: narrator; intelligent, highly respected Professor of the Paris Museum; adventurous spirit becomes evident as he views the wonderful underwater world he encounters aboard the *Nautilus*

Captain Nemo: brilliant, embittered, cynical, vindictive commander of the *Nautilus*; intends to keep Aronnax, Conseil, and Land captives in order to maintain secrecy about his submarine

Conseil: Aronnax's loyal, unassertive servant who uncomplainingly accompanies him on all his adventures

Ned Land: Canadian; excellent harpooner; ordinarily impassive but becomes disgruntled and spends his time plotting to escape during the long voyage

Captain Farragut: commander of the *Abraham Lincoln*, the ship commissioned by the United States government to rid the seas of the monster that has been attacking ships

Captain Anders: commander of the *Scotia*

Crew of the *Nautilus*: unnamed outcasts from different countries of the world; completely loyal to Captain Nemo

About the Author

Jules Verne was born February 8, 1828, in Nantes, France. In 1847, he began studying law in Paris, but his passion for writing superceded his desire to practice law. He began to write plays and opera lyrics in 1848 and had his first play published in 1850. His first novel, *Five Weeks in a Balloon*, was published in 1863 and foreshadowed his success as an author of fantasy, adventure, and science. Other major works include *Journey to the Center of the Earth* (1864), *From the Earth to the Moon* (1866), *Twenty Thousand Leagues Under the Sea* (1870), *Around the World in Eighty Days* (1873), *Mysterious Island* (1874), and *Master of the World* (1904). In addition to writing fantasy and adventure stories, he wrote several historical novels, including *North Against South* (1887). His works include sixty-five novels, thirty plays, several short stories and essays, and some opera librettos and geographical works. Regarded as the "Father of Science Fiction," Verne's writing takes his readers over, above, and beneath the earth. He envisioned and wrote about scientific achievements of the twentieth century, including airplanes, submarines, rocket ships, satellites, guided missiles, and the development of radio, motion pictures, and television. In 1857 Verne married Honorine Morel, a young widow with two daughters. Verne's only biological child, Michel, was born in 1861. Jules Verne died in 1905.

Background Information

1. Movies: Several movie versions of the book have been produced. Some distort the story considerably. An excellent silent version was produced in 1916 and has been newly obtained from an archive print. The most well-known was produced by Disney in 1954: 127 min.; directed by Richard Fleisher; stars James Mason as Nemo, Paul Lucas as Aronnax, Peter Lorre as Conseil, and Kirk Douglas as Ned Land; won Oscars for Art Direction and Special Effects. Additional information about movie versions can be found online.

2. Verne named his imaginary submarine the *Nautilus* after Robert Fulton's invention of a diving boat (1801) that could descend twenty-five feet underwater. In 1886 two Englishmen built the first all-electric submarine and named it *Nautilus* in honor of Verne's vessel. In 1954, the United States Navy launched the first nuclear-powered submarine, the *Nautilus*. This vessel broke all previous submarine records for underwater speed and endurance and in 1958 became the first submarine to sail under the ice at the North Pole. After traveling almost half a million miles over a span of twenty-five years, the vessel was decommissioned in 1980. The submarine was designated as a National Historic Landmark in 1982 and is on public exhibit in Groton, Connecticut.

3. Prepare an overhead transparency to introduce the following terms. (a) league: a measure of distance equaling about 3 geographical miles, 3.452 statute miles, or 4.8280 kilometers (b) fathom: unit of measure, equal to 6 feet, used to measure the depth of water (c) nautical mile: the standard unit of distance in nautical measure, 6,076.11549 feet (d) knot: measure of speed for ships, one nautical mile per hour; i.e., A ship with 20-knot speed can go 20 nautical miles an hour.

4. Sea creatures mentioned in the book—1. cetacean (p. 9): any one of an order of marine animals characterized by fishlike, almost hairless bodies, flat, notched tails and paddle-shaped forelimbs, e.g., whales, dolphins, porpoises 2. narwhal (p. 15): toothed whale of the arctic seas; male has a long, slender, twisted tusk from 6 to 10 feet long that extends forward 3. squid (p. 23): sea animal like an octopus, having 10 arms instead of 8 and a pair of tail fins 4. whale (p. 26): mammal shaped like a huge fish, with a broad, flat tail, flippers, and no hind limbs 5. sea-spider (p. 85): any one of a group of spider-like marine arthropods

6. sea-otter (p. 87): large otter with webbed feet 7. dogfish (p. 88): any one of several kinds of small sharks 8. oyster (p. 137): kind of mollusk having a rough, irregular shell in two halves 9. shark (p. 137): any one of a group of fishes having streamlined, spindle-like bodies, certain kinds of which are large and ferocious 10. cachalots (p. 197): large, toothed whales having square heads 11. cephalopod (p. 238): any one of the most highly organized class of marine mollusks, characterized by long, arm-like tentacles around the mouth, a large head, a sharp beak, and a siphon used in propulsion, e.g., squids, octopuses

5. The Latin meaning for "Nemo" is "no one."

Initiating Activities

Use one or more of the following to introduce the novel.

1. Have students research reported sightings of sea monsters, e.g., the Loch Ness Monster. Have students write an essay in which they identify and give information about three "monsters," including description, location, and era of sightings, and whether or not the true identity was ever discovered.

2. Place the phrase "Twenty Thousand Leagues Under the Sea" on an overhead transparency. Elicit students' responses, e.g., those who have heard of or read the book, possible connotations of the phrase, and possible content of the book.

3. Read aloud the "teasers" on the back cover, then preview the book. Brainstorm with students about the title, the author, the cover illustration, when the book was written, and the titles of the chapters.

4. Have a map on display and trace the voyage of the *Nautilus* (see page 69 of the novel for the beginning of the journey).

5. Show selected clips from the 1954 Disney movie version.

6. Place the word "adventure" on an overhead transparency. Elicit students' responses concerning synonyms, antonyms, situations they expect to find in an adventure novel, and adventures in which they have participated.

7. Have students keep a journal of questions to ask in class as they read.

8. Have students create their own glossary of unfamiliar words as they read.

Character Web

Directions: Choose a character from the novel and complete the chart below. Cite evidence from the story as you fill in information.

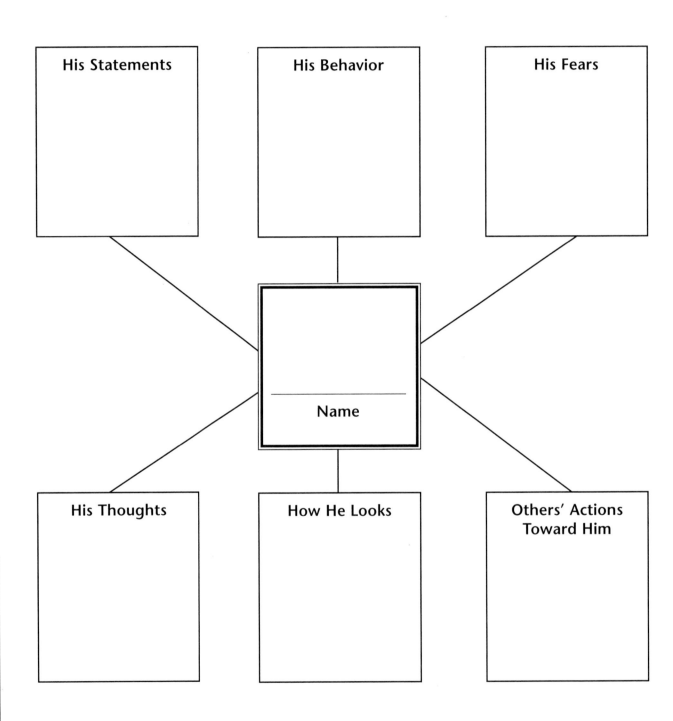

His Statements

His Behavior

His Fears

Name

His Thoughts

How He Looks

Others' Actions Toward Him

Using Predictions

We all make predictions as we read—little guesses about what will happen next, how a conflict will be resolved, which details will be important to the plot, which details will help fill in our sense of a character. Students should be encouraged to predict, to make sensible guesses as they read the novel.

As students work on their predictions, these discussion questions can be used to guide them: What are some of the ways to predict? What is the process of a sophisticated reader's thinking and predicting? What clues does an author give to help us make predictions? Why are some predictions more likely to be accurate than others?

Create a chart for recording predictions. This could either be an individual or class activity. As each subsequent chapter is discussed, students can review and correct their previous predictions about plot and characters as necessary.

Use the facts and ideas the author gives.

Use your own prior knowledge.

Apply any new information (i.e., from class discussion) that may cause you to change your mind.

Predictions

_____

_____

_____

_____

Prediction Chart

What characters have we met so far?	What is the conflict in the story?	What are your predictions?	Why did you make these predictions?

Character Chart

Directions: In the boxes across from each of the feelings, describe an incident or time in the book when each of the listed characters experienced that feeling. You may use "not applicable" if you cannot find an example.

	Captain Nemo	Professor Aronnax	Conseil	Ned Land
Frustration				
Anger				
Fear				
Humiliation				
Relief				

Story Map

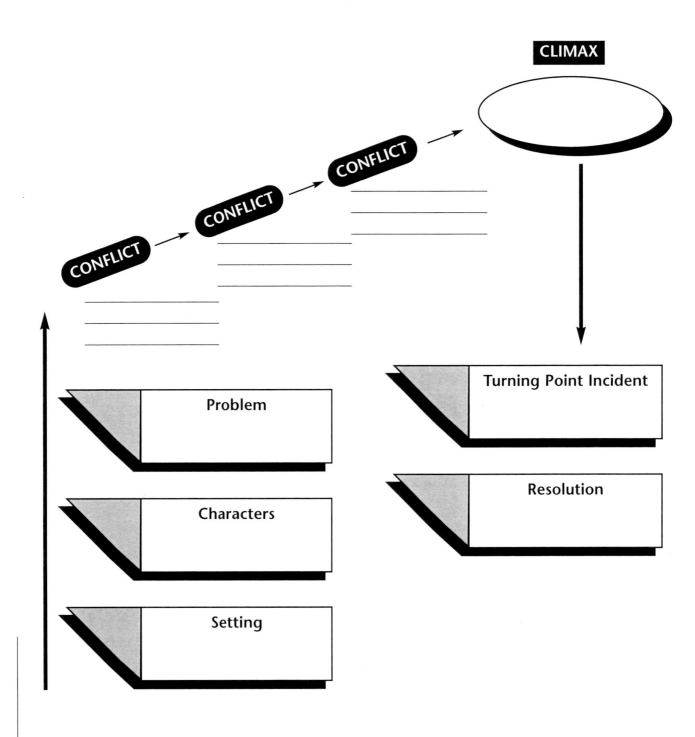

Story Map

Directions: Select five important events from the novel and put them sequentially into this flow chart. Be sure to choose events that cover the plot through the last chapter.

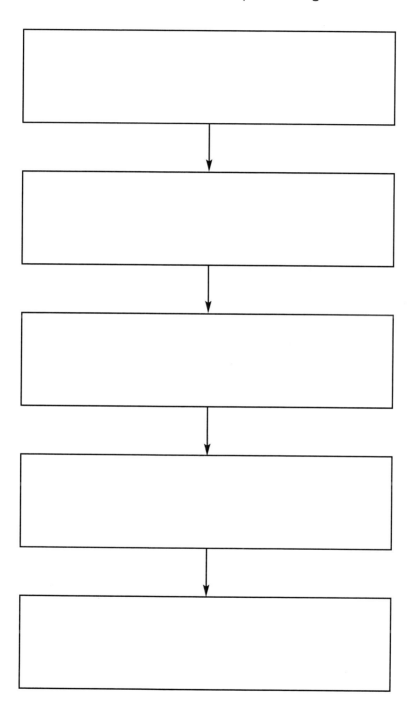

Thematic Analysis

Directions: Choose a theme from the book to be the focus of your word web. Complete the web and then answer the question in each starred box.

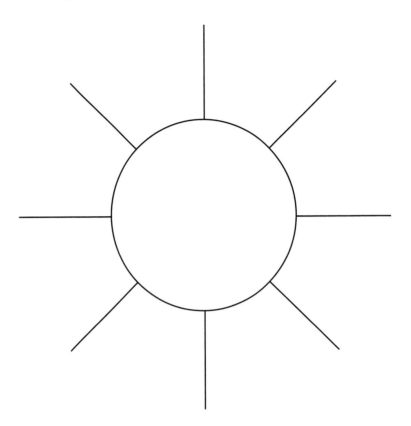

 What is the author's main message?

 What did you learn from the book?

Venn Diagram

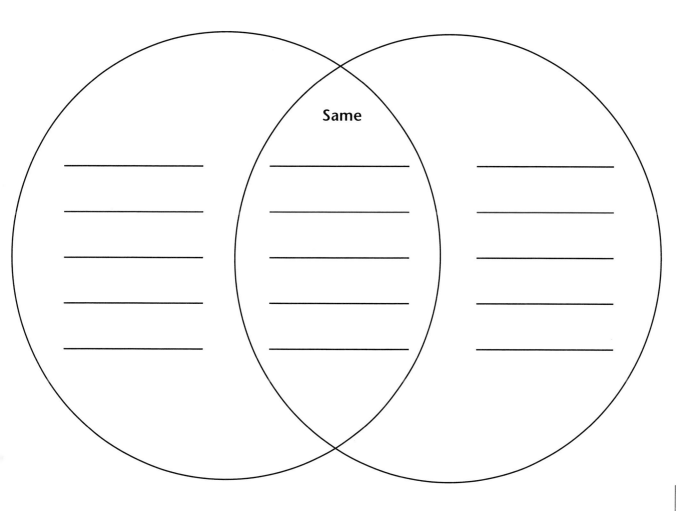

Same

Note: Examples of literary devices found in each section are included in the Supplementary Activities. Guide students to identify these devices as they read the novel. Some sections include an Enrichment Activity for accelerated students.

Part One, Chapters 1–5, pp. 9–28

After a mysterious underwater monster attacks several ocean ships, the public demands action. Authorities consult Professor Aronnax, who has been on a scientific tour in the United States. He is asked to join an expedition to search for and destroy the monster.

Vocabulary
inexplicable (9)
impunity (11)
prodigious (12)
formidable (12)
enigma (14)
veritable (18)
savants (18)

Discussion Questions

1. Examine information about the phenomenon that causes excitement and speculation on two continents. *(Seafaring people and government officials in Europe and America are excited by news of the mysterious "monster" ships are meeting. It is long, spindle-shaped, sometimes phosphorescent, larger and faster than a whale, and can function in warm or cold water. Controversy surrounds tales of the monster and questions abound about whether or not the problem is scientific or legendary. The problem becomes a real danger when the monster begins to attack ships, and the public demands a solution. pp. 9–12)*

2. Discuss the incidents involving the *Moravian* and the *Scotia* and examine the ensuing publicity. *(While sailing in the Atlantic Ocean, the* Moravian *strikes an unexplained, uncharted "rock" and endangers the lives of all aboard. Something sharp strikes the* Scotia, *causing a large hole, and water fills one of the compartments. Examination of the damage reveals a triangular-shaped tear caused by a penetrating object, which was then withdrawn in a backward movement. A fearful public demands that the seas be rid of this monster, now thought to be either a huge monster or a powerful submarine. pp. 10–12)*

3. Discuss the information Professor Aronnax reveals about himself. *(He is the Professor of the Paris Museum and has been on a scientific tour in the United States. He has read about and is puzzled by the mystery but has not formed a conclusion. He has gained respect by his published work,* The Mysteries of the Great Submarine Grounds, *and is asked by the* New York Herald *to give his opinion about the phenomenon in the seas. pp. 13–14)*

4. Examine the information in Aronnax's article, the conclusion he draws about the monster, and the results of his article. Discuss the cause and effect in this section. *(Cause: Aronnax is asked to state his opinion about the sea monster. He writes an article explaining that he has examined different theories about the monster and believes they are dealing with an extraordinary marine animal. He gives two theories. (a) Because no one has explored the greatest depths of the ocean, no one knows about creatures that live there. One of them has possibly surfaced. (b) If the creature is one of the identified species, he believes it is a colossal narwhal, also known as the sea-unicorn. If the narwhal is five-to-ten times larger than ordinary, its tusk could be strong enough to cause the damage done to the* Scotia. *This is the theory Aronnax proposes. Effects: (a) His article is well received and much discussed by the public. (b) The* Abraham Lincoln *is commissioned to search for and destroy the monster, but it delays its departure because no one knows where to search. Cause: The creature strikes again, this time in the Pacific Ocean. Effects: (a) The* Abraham Lincoln *prepares to depart immediately. (b) Professor Aronnax is asked to join the expedition. pp. 13–17)*

5. Discuss Conseil and analyze his characteristics. Why is he important for Aronnax's mission? *(Conseil, a Dutchman, is Aronnax's faithful servant. For ten years, he has accompanied Aronnax on all his journeys. He is brave, loyal, calm, punctual, and zealous. He is unruffled by life's surprises, skillful with his hands, uncomplaining, and never gives advice unless asked. His only flaw is that he is intensely formal and only speaks to Aronnax in the third person, "monsieur." Importance: He will attend to all the preparations for the voyage and will support Aronnax in anything he requires of him. pp. 18–20)*

6. Discuss Captain Farragut and Ned Land and compare/contrast their reactions to stories of the monster with Arronax's reaction. *(Farragut is commander of the* Abraham Lincoln. *He is a good seaman who is the "soul" of his ship. He and his men believe emphatically in the existence of the sea-unicorn, and he prepares his ship to seize the creature. Farragut offers $2,000 to the first man to signal the presence of the monster. Land is a skillful Canadian harpooner who has been hired by Farragut for the voyage. He is 40 years old, tall, strong, calm, stubborn, and reserved. Land is the only person on the ship who does not believe in the narwhal. Aronnax repeats his belief that the monster is a powerful, organized sea mammal. pp. 21–24)*

7. Analyze the attitude of the *Abraham Lincoln's* crew after three months at sea. Do you think you would feel the same way? *(The men are embarrassed and angry. They regret missing meals and spending so much time looking for the creature. They become indifferent to their duties and want to return home. Aronnax begins to think he and Conseil have wasted their time. Farragut agrees to return to port if they do not sight the monster in three days; Responses will vary. pp. 26–28)*

8. How does Aronnax try to convince Land that the creature is real? *(Aronnax portrays the creature as being powerfully organized. He says it must have incalculable strength, the necessary structure to remain in and resist the pressure of deep water, and exceptional speed. Land comments that it must be made of iron plates eight inches thick, but says that the Scotia's accident is not true. pp. 24–25)*

9. **Prediction:** Do you think Land or Aronnax's belief is correct? Explain your response.

Supplementary Activities

1. Research/Writing: As a class, research large sea animals. Ask: Do any seem strong enough to match the description in the novel? Have students defend their answers in a few paragraphs.

2. Creative Writing: Based on the attributes of Conseil, have students write a short poem or paragraph about a friend who has some of the same attributes.

3. Creative Writing: Conseil is loyal to Aronnax in the novel. Have students write a metaphor or simile poem about "loyalty." Pattern—Line 1: noun; Lines 2–4: write something about the subject, with each line saying something different and giving an idea of what the subject is like; Line 5: a metaphor or simile that begins with the title.

4. Literary Devices: Guide students to find and list a simile and a metaphor from each section. This will be an ongoing assignment throughout the book. Some examples are given for each reading section. **Similes**—"tusk...as hard as steel;" [tusks] "pierced...through like a gimlet in a barrel" (p. 15); **Metaphor**—Captain Farragut: telescope, cannon (p. 22); **Allusion**—Moby Dick (p. 10)

Chapters 6–9, pp. 29–52

The *Abraham Lincoln* pursues the monster and comes within 1,000 feet of it. The ship is damaged after Land attempts to harpoon the creature. Aronnax falls overboard, Conseil dives in to save him, and they discover that Land has also fallen overboard. All three are taken captive aboard the mysterious creature, a sea vessel, where they are treated hospitably.

Vocabulary
malediction (34)
indefatigably (34)
abyss (36)
imperturbable (37)
vertiginous (40)
infamous (46)
implacable (52)

Discussion Questions

1. Discuss the sea monster and the reaction to it by the crew of the *Abraham Lincoln*. *(It lies several feet below the surface of the water and gives off a mysterious light that reveals a huge, elongated oval. The crew is filled with disbelief, amazement, and fear. They try to escape, but the monster pursues with incredible speed, turns off its lights, then reappears on the other side of the ship. The monster remains close all night, and after emitting a deafening whistle, it submerges. pp. 29–31)*

2. Examine Ned Land's conclusions about the amazing events and then describe what happens next. *(Based on the roaring whistle, Land believes they have encountered a large whale. The creature reappears at 2:00 a.m. and remains about five miles away. The crew observes a "monster" about 150 feet long, spouting vapor fifty yards high. The* Abraham Lincoln *prepares for combat and heads straight for the creature but is unable to overtake it, even after Captain Farragut orders more pressure. The chase continues throughout the day. When the creature reappears at night, the frigate approaches noiselessly to within 20 feet of its adversary, and Land fires a harpoon, which seems to strike a hard body. During the shock that follows, Aronnax falls into the sea. pp. 30–35)*

3. Discuss what happens to Aronnax and analyze what Conseil's reaction reveals about him. *(After falling into the sea, Aronnax almost drowns. Conseil, who dove into the water when his master fell in, saves his life. He reveals to Aronnax that the frigate is damaged and cannot return to rescue them. Throughout the night, Aronnax and Conseil swim together. When Aronnax becomes too exhausted to continue, Conseil holds him up, vowing to drown with him rather than desert him. Conseil continues to call for help; Responses will vary. pp. 36–38)*

4. Discuss Ned Land's reappearance and examine what he tells Aronnax and Conseil about the creature. *(Ned Land stands on a "floating island." He has found the giant narwhal they have been pursuing. Land assists the two men aboard. He tells them that the "beast" is made of sheet-iron plates, and they realize the creature is manmade. Land has seen no sign of life for the three hours he has been clinging to the vessel. pp. 38–40)*

5. Discuss how the three men escape from the ocean waters. Note the irony of the trio's situation. *(When the vessel begins to submerge, Land kicks the metal and cries out. The sinking stops, a man raises an iron plate and sees the three men, then eight men drag the trio into the vessel. Irony: The men have become captives of the creature they have been pursuing. pp. 41–42)*

6. Examine the interaction of the captives with the first two men who appear. *(After remaining in the dark for some time, the cabin is filled with light. Two men appear. One is short and muscular; the other is tall and self-confident and seems to be the one in charge. He is between 35 and 50 years old, appears calm, energetic, and courageous, and has tremendous vision. Aronnax realizes that he is the commander of the vessel. He examines the captives attentively, then speaks to his companion in a language Aronnax does not understand. He does not respond in any language the trio speaks to him. Land becomes furious when the two men leave without establishing verbal*

communication. A servant enters with food. An "N" is engraved on the plates, the first clue to the identity of their captor. pp. 42–47)

7. Examine the way in which each of the men reacts to his captivity. *(Ned Land is angry and complains because a second meal has not arrived. His one goal is to escape. Conseil sees no benefit in complaining and remains calm and complaisant. Aronnax is logical and believes they have become aware of an important secret. He believes they must remain calm and do nothing for the present. Land concedes and promises not to accept the situation without becoming enraged, but announces his plans to find a way to escape, even if it means seizing the vessel. After no one comes for hours, Aronnax concludes that their captor is cruel and may plan to starve them to death. Land seizes the steward when he arrives with food, and Conseil intervenes. pp. 47–52)*

8. **Prediction:** Aronnax and Conseil are mostly positive when they first board the submarine. By the end of this section, Aronnax is not sure about their captor. What do you think will happen? Explain your answer.

Supplementary Activities

1. Drama: Working in small groups, have students stage one scene from this section, e.g., Aronnax and Conseil's struggle to survive, Ned Land's appearance, the men's first experience as captives, the morning after their capture.

2. Newspaper Writing: Have students write a newspaper article written after the *Abraham Lincoln* returns to port without the three men.

3. Literary Devices: **Similes**—[garments] "dragged me down like a leaden weight" (p. 37) "This hole's as dark as one [an oven];" "light that shone around the submarine boat like a magnificent phosphoric phenomenon" (p. 43); **Metaphors**—ocean: billowy cradle (p. 35) the submarine: floating island (p. 40)

Chapters 10–12, pp. 53–79

Captain Nemo reveals to the captives that they are on a submarine, and he will not permit them to leave. However, Arronax and his companions are provided for and given full access to the submarine, called the *Nautilus*. They are intrigued by the mechanical structure and elegance of the vessel and by the mysteries under the sea. Land plots their escape.

Vocabulary
despots (58)
vivacity (73)

Discussion Questions

1. Examine Captain Nemo's first conversation with his captives, its implications for them, and what this reveals about him. What do you think happened in Captain Nemo's personal history? *(He reveals that he speaks several languages but chose not to respond during his first visit so that he could ponder what to do with them. Nemo seems to have broken all ties with humanity and the laws of men. Aronnax informs him of the problems his vessel has caused in Europe and America. Nemo says he has the right to treat the captives as enemies, he owes them no hospitality, and he could abandon them in the sea from where they came. In exchange for their liberty aboard the vessel, he imposes one condition: they must be willing to stay in their cabin for hours or days. In response to Aronnax's question, Nemo tells them they must forever renounce the idea of seeing their country, friends, or relatives again. Reactions: Aronnax is intrigued by thoughts of study and observation. Conseil always agrees with his master. Land is angry and vows he will try to escape; Responses will vary. pp. 53–59)*

2. Discuss what Aronnax discovers aboard the *Nautilus* and its effect on him. *(The library of 12,000 books contains books on many subjects, written in every language, but does not have even one book on political economy. The newest volume, published in 1865, indicates the time Nemo retreated from the world. Aronnax discovers a museum filled with treasures of nature and art worth millions of dollars. Captain Nemo discloses that he had once been a collector of art and ancient relics. A large organ holds works of eminent composers. Elegant glass cases hold priceless treasures of the sea. As an academic, Aronnax is delighted by everything he sees. pp. 60–63)*

3. Examine details about the operations of the *Nautilus* and its equipment. *(The vessel is powered by electricity that Nemo extracts from the chemical elements of the sea. It has two hulls, making the vessel resistant to projectiles and unimaginable pressure at the depths of the ocean. It fills its reservoirs with water to descend, then expels the water when it reaches the surface to renew its supply of oxygen. Using innovative techniques, the helmsman, who is placed in a glass cage jutting from the top, can steer the vessel horizontally or vertically. The rays from a powerful electric refractor light up the ocean's depths for half a mile. It is designed to withstand natural and manmade catastrophes. Under various aliases, Nemo had each separate portion of the* Nautilus *built in different parts of the world, then he and others put it together on a desert island. He loves his vessel as if it were his own flesh. pp. 64–67)*

4. Analyze Aronnax's reaction to Captain Nemo and the wonders of the *Nautilus.* *(He is puzzled by what could have caused such vengeance as Nemo displays. Even though Land continues to plot ways to escape, Aronnax acknowledges his reluctance to escape before seeing the wonders of the* Nautilus. *Aronnax, Conseil, and Land are amazed at the wondrous sights as the windows of the submarine reveal the wonders of the ocean's depths, which they observe for two hours. pp. 69–73)*

5. Discuss the type of hunt on which the captives are invited to accompany Captain Nemo. *(Aronnax discovers that the forest on the island of Crespo, where they will hunt, is submarine rather than terrestrial. They must dress in diving apparatus, and they will use air guns that project glass percussion caps, which are actually small glass bulbs from which electricity is forced at high tension. pp. 76–79)*

Supplementary Activities

1. Art: Have students sketch their impression of the *Nautilus* or bring to class pictures of submarines to compare with the description of the *Nautilus.*

2. Literary Devices: **Similes**—"like a balloon into the air" (p. 65) "He did love his vessel like a father loves his child!" (p. 66); "It is like being at an aquarium" (p. 72); **Metaphor**—the *Nautilus*: iron prison (p. 71); **Allusion**—Orpheus, a musician in Greek and Roman mythology (p. 62)

Chapters 13–16, pp. 80–101

Aronnax and Conseil accompany Nemo on an underwater hunt and explore the depths of the ocean. The *Nautilus* approaches a wrecked ship with corpses. The vessel later enters the dangerous Torres Straits. The captives receive permission from Nemo to explore an island.

Vocabulary
ironical (81)
contiguous (82)
voracious (89)
Protestant (95)
complaisant (99)

Discussion Questions

1. Discuss preparations for the underwater exploration. Note the reactions of Conseil and Ned Land to accompanying Aronnax and what this reveals about each of them. *(Nemo has invited the men to go with him and has provided the necessary clothing for the excursion. They will explore the submarine forests of Crespo Island. Land is disappointed that the hunt will be underwater and refuses to go. Conseil will follow Aronnax wherever he goes. Land reveals his obstinate, inflexible approach to any situation. Conseil reveals his loyalty to and trust in his master. Nemo, his companion, Aronnax, and Conseil prepare for the adventure. pp. 80–82)*

2. Examine details about the underwater hunt and its effect on Aronnax. *(Aronnax is enthralled with the underwater world from the beginning of the trip to the end. They walk on fine sand and meadows of seaweed to a depth of 300 feet, where they reach the borders of the forest of Crespo Island. After meeting a dangerous sea-spider, they reach the island of Crespo but cannot climb its enormous granite cliffs. On their return to the* Nautilus *by a different route, Nemo kills a magnificent sea otter, and his companion kills a large albatross that hovers above the water. Shortly before reaching the* Nautilus, *the men fall to the ground and lie motionless to avoid two fierce dogfish. Land regrets not going when Conseil tells him of the ocean's wonders. pp. 82–89, 93)*

3. Discuss the significance of Aronnax's additional discoveries. Why do you think the submarine comes so close to a sunken ship? *(Twenty sailors, apparently from different nations, come on deck and retrieve nets filled with hundreds of pounds of fish. Nemo reveals his love for and knowledge of the ocean and alludes to his belief that future nautical towns could exist. Aronnax and Nemo observe a sunken ship with corpses still visible. The scene numbs both men as they observe sharks heading toward the human flesh; Responses will vary. pp. 90–94)*

4. The author describes the corpses on the ship in great detail. Why do you think he does this? *(Responses will vary. Suggestion: Jules Verne wants the readers to understand how awful the sight is for Aronnax and his companions.)*

5. Examine the conflicting attitudes of Conseil and Land toward their captivity aboard the *Nautilus*. Which attitude would you most likely share? *(Conseil wishes Aronnax a happy New Year, stating that they may never have another occasion to see sights such as they have seen aboard the* Nautilus *and that he would be happy to see everything in the new year. Conseil thinks as much about remaining on the submarine as Land does about escaping. Conseil wants whatever will please his master. Land concentrates on escaping and believes the opportunity has come when the* Nautilus *runs aground in a coral reef in the Torres Straits. Aronnax, however, realizes the perils of attempting to escape across the lands of New Guinea; Responses will vary. pp. 95–101)*

6. Discuss the importance of the captives' excursion to an island and the man most affected by it. *(They are surprised and elated when Nemo allows them to go ashore on an island. This is the first time the men have been allowed to leave the* Nautilus *while on the surface of the ocean. Ned Land, overjoyed, feels that he is a prisoner escaping from a prison. In addition, he has an opportunity to eat something besides fish, i.e., meat. pp. 100–101)*

7. Analyze the irony of Nemo's statement, "Our voyage is only just begun, and I do not wish to deprive myself so soon of the honour of your company." *(Aronnax is Nemo's prisoner; yet, he speaks as if Aronnax is his honored guest and can leave when he wishes. Nemo assumes the honor is mutual. p. 98)*

8. **Prediction:** What will happen to the three men on the island?

Supplementary Activities

1. Writing/Art: Have students do one of the following: Complete the statement, "Contentment is..." based on Conseil's attitude, or sketch one scene from the underwater excursion.

2. Literary Devices: **Similes**—"...head shook like an almond in its shell" (p. 82) "fish-flies flew...like a swarm of humming-birds" (p. 85); **Metaphor**—ocean floor: dazzling carpet (p. 83)

Chapters 17–18, pp. 102–115

The captives explore the Island of Gilboa. They collect coconuts, bread-tree fruit, and other fruits. They return the next day to hunt. Natives attack them and then surround the *Nautilus* after the trio returns to the submarine. The natives are repelled by electricity from the submarine.

Vocabulary

circumspection (105)
middling (106)
ecstasy (109)
pirogues (111)
equilibrium (111)
frigate (112)
vociferations (114)
gambols (114)

Discussion Questions

1. Discuss what happens while the captives are on land and the effects of the experience on each of the men. *(They all welcome the chance to walk on land again and relish the abundant fresh fruit. Land is determined to find game to eat. They return to the* Nautilus, *but make a second trip to the Island of Gilboa the next day and explore further inland. They obtain some meat when Conseil and Land kill some pigeons, a hog, and some small kangaroos. The trio discusses staying on the island instead of returning to the* Nautilus, *but their conversation is interrupted when natives attack them. pp. 102–108).*

2. The author of the novel uses the term "savages" to describe the natives of the island. Discuss why the author uses this term. *(Responses will vary.)*

3. Examine details of the conflict with the natives and what this reveals about Nemo and his submarine. *(Aronnax, Conseil, and Land reach the submarine safely, but by morning several hundred natives have attacked it. The natives assemble in canoes, surround the submarine, and begin to shoot arrows toward it, but Nemo remains calm and shuts the submarine's panels. When the panels are opened the next morning, many of the natives are onboard. As they attempt to enter, they receive an electrical shock from the hand-rail and retreat in terror. pp. 108–115)*

4. Analyze evidence of Nemo's character in this and the prior section. *(Responses will vary; Suggestions—He shows cynicism in his belief that the earth needs new men, not new continents. His bitterness and his determination are obvious in his vow that nothing can force him to set foot on land again. He demonstrates confidence in himself when he allows his captives to go to the island alone and in his ship when he is not disturbed by the threat of the natives. He shows compassion when he puts only enough electricity through the hand-rail to frighten the natives rather than to kill them. pp. 95, 98, 109, 114)*

Supplementary Activities

1. Character Analysis: Have students compare and contrast the men's impression of the natives, from the perspectives of Nemo vs. Aronnax, Conseil, or Land.

2. Literary Devices: **Simile**—"The *Nautilus* [emerged from the waves] like a long rock" (p. 106); **Metaphor**—arrows: hail (p. 111)

Chapters 19–20, pp. 116–128

Captain Nemo confines the captives to their rooms for unspecified reasons. Nemo asks Aronnax to treat a man of his crew, who ultimately dies from a horrible wound and is buried in an undersea tomb.

Vocabulary
interdicted (118)
imperious (118)
soporific (120)
morbid (120)
physiognomy (122)
spasmodic (123)
inextricable (125)

Discussion Questions

1. Examine events of January 18 and their effect on Aronnax. *(The* Nautilus *surfaces after traveling underwater for several days. Aronnax goes to the platform to observe their surroundings when Nemo appears, scans the horizon with his telescope, then speaks to his officer. Both are perturbed about something they see. When Aronnax attempts to look through his telescope, Nemo angrily snatches the telescope and orders Aronnax and the other captives to stay in their rooms. The men find food prepared, and shortly after they dine, the lights go out and leave them in profound darkness. Aronnax realizes they have been drugged to ensure a deep sleep. pp. 116–120)*

2. Discuss the implications of the next meeting between Aronnax and Nemo. *(Aronnax awakens the next morning with no negative effects of the drug. They are on the surface of the sea, which is deserted, and nothing aboard the* Nautilus *seems changed. Nemo appears in the afternoon, looking fatigued and deeply sorrowful. After Nemo confirms that Aronnax is a doctor and a surgeon, Nemo asks him to follow. There is a man who has suffered a horrible wound to his skull and is approaching death. Nemo says the man was struck by a lever. Nemo is overcome with emotion when Aronnax tells him that he can do nothing to help the man, who will die within two hours. Aronnax leaves, and Nemo remains with the dying man. pp. 121–124)*

3. Discuss the underwater excursion the captives make with Nemo. Note the implications of his final remarks. *(At Nemo's request, they join him the morning after the crewman's death. Aronnax is amazed at the beauty as they descend into the depths of the "kingdom of coral." Nemo stops, and Aronnax and his companions observe four crewmen carrying an oblong object. Aronnax realizes the group has reached an undersea cemetery, defined by a coral cross in the center, and the object is the body of the crewman. The men dig a grave in the coral, bury the man, and kneel in prayer. The funeral procession returns to the* Nautilus. *Nemo reveals his bitterness toward humans when he says that the crewman is out of the reach of sharks and men. pp. 121–128)*

4. **Prediction:** Will Nemo prove to be trustworthy? Explain your response.

Supplementary Activities

1. Drama/Writing/Interview: Divide the class into three groups. Have each group take one scene (as identified in questions 1–3) and portray this to the class via a skit, a poem, or an interview with one of the men involved.

2. Literary Device: **Metaphor**—the three captives: snails (p. 116)

Part Two, Chapters 1–4, pp. 131–155

The *Nautilus* begins the second part of its voyage. Aronnax realizes Nemo uses his submarine as an instrument of revenge. Land continues to plan their escape. Nemo takes the captives to an oyster-bank. The *Nautilus* travels from the Red Sea to the Mediterranean via an underwater tunnel.

Vocabulary
disdain (131)
crypt (143)
foliated (144)
limpidity (144)
opaque (147)
audacious (147)
labyrinth (150)
ulterior (152)
epoch (152)
subterranean (153)

Discussion Questions

1. Analyze Aronnax's changing attitude toward Nemo. Compare this with that of Conseil. (*Although he recognizes Nemo as a misunderstood genius, his actions before and following the crewman's death have given Aronnax a different perspective. He now believes that Nemo desires revenge on human society and that he has prepared the* Nautilus *to perpetrate that revenge. He realizes that nothing binds the captives to Nemo. They may be addressed as guests, but they are prisoners, and Nemo has control. Aronnax struggles with whether to hate or admire Nemo, yet he still wants to observe the marvels of the ocean. Conseil believes Nemo seeks refuge in the ocean because it is the only place he can exercise his natural talents and abilities. pp. 131–132*)

2. Discuss Land's plans and how they conflict with Aronnax's. (*He continues with his plans to escape. He believes the time has come as the* Nautilus *approaches Keeling Island. Aronnax, who has an insatiable desire to learn, suggests waiting to escape until the ship is nearer Europe because he secretly wants to experience everything he can aboard the* Nautilus. *pp. 132–134*)

3. Discuss Nemo's "fresh proposition" and the response of the three captives. (*Nemo invites the captives to go with him to an oyster bank. At first Aronnax agrees but is afraid and has nightmares after Nemo mentions sharks. Aronnax hopes Conseil will provide him a way out by refusing, but both he and Land don't know about the sharks at first and envision finding magnificent pearls. When they do learn of the sharks, Land relishes the prospect of nabbing a shark with his harpoon, and Conseil wants to face whatever his master faces. pp. 135–140*)

4. Examine details of the excursion to the oyster bank. Analyze what this trip discloses about Captain Nemo. (*The group goes by boat to the landing point near Manaar Island, along the western coast of Ceylon. Nemo and the three captives dress in diving apparatus and descend, armed with blades. Land also carries a harpoon. Nemo leads the men into a cave, where they observe an extraordinarily large oyster with a pearl as large as a coconut, of perfect clarity and immeasurable value. Aronnax realizes that Nemo is the only one who knows about this pearl. pp. 140–145*)

5. Discuss what the men encounter as they return to the boat and the consequences of this meeting. (*On their return to the boat, the men see an Indian diver searching for oysters, but he does not see them. They watch him go up and plunge several times, retrieving only a few oysters each time. He suddenly exhibits great fear, and the men observe an enormous, voracious shark advancing toward him. The shark strikes the diver with his tail, knocking him to the ground. Nemo advances, the shark throws Nemo back, but Nemo thrusts his dagger into its stomach, then engages in combat with the shark. Just as it seems the shark has won and is about to clamp its jaws on Nemo, Ned Land strikes the monster's heart with his harpoon and kills it. Land frees the captain, who in turn frees the Indian, and all of them reach the diver's boat. Nemo and Conseil revive the diver, and Nemo puts a bag of pearls into his hand, leaving the diver behind as they return to the oyster bank. pp. 145–148*)

6. Analyze what the battle reveals about Nemo and Land. What do you think Land's final remark to Nemo means? *(Nemo thanks Land, who replies that he owed it to him, i.e., repayment for Nemo saving his life. Aronnax later reflects on two observations: Nemo's courage and the way he jeopardized his own life to save the diver. When Aronnax mentions this to Nemo, he replies that the diver inhabits the same oppressed country as he. Nemo reveals a compassion for oppressed people and bitterness toward a country that oppresses its inhabitants. He says that his native country will never be different. pp. 148–149)*

7. Examine the opinions of the captives regarding the possibility of entering the Mediterranean Sea from the Red Sea and the actuality of the trip. [Note: The Suez Canal was opened in 1869; the *Nautilus* is in the Red Sea in February 1868.] *(Because the Suez Canal is not yet opened [p. 152], there is no channel between the Red Sea and the Mediterranean Sea. Land and Aronnax speculate that the submarine will go from the Persian Gulf back to the Indian Ocean and eventually to the Cape of Good Hope. After the* Nautilus *enters the Red Sea, Aronnax cannot believe when Nemo tells him they will be in the Mediterranean the day after tomorrow. He believes it is impossible for the submarine to travel fast enough to go around Africa to get to the Mediterranean. Nemo takes the* Nautilus *through a submarine tunnel. Aronnax watches Nemo steer the submarine through the channel. pp. 150–154)*

8. Analyze Aronnax's statement, "…I was so fond of the *Nautilus* that I rowed in the same boat as its commander." *(Aronnax rejects Land's suggestion that they try to escape. He does not want the voyage to end yet because it offers him a chance to see things most men have not seen. He seems to share Nemo's fondness for the* Nautilus. *p. 151)*

9. Analyze the insinuation of Nemo's statement to Aronnax, "…there can be no secret between people who are never to leave each other again" (p. 154). Why do you think Aronnax leaves this out when telling the other captives of his conversation with Nemo? *(Nemo has no intention of releasing his captives and believes they have no chance to escape; Responses will vary. Suggestion: Aronnax does not want to further upset Land.)*

Supplementary Activities
1. Analysis/Presentation: Working in small groups, have students decide what country Nemo is from and what happened to him there, then write a brief explanation to share with the class.

2. Literary Devices: **Simile**—"pearl as large as a coconut" (p. 144); **Metaphor**—pearl: fruit of Nature (p. 144); **Allusion**—Cleopatra (p. 138)

Chapters 5–6, pp. 156–180
Aronnax and Land have different opinions about the timing of an escape, but Aronnax finally agrees to Land's escape plan. Nemo's actions are increasingly mystifying. The *Nautilus* reaches the Atlantic Ocean. Aronnax discovers the source of Nemo's wealth.

Vocabulary
annihilate (159)
hermetically (161)
taciturn (161)
infinite (173)
mortal (175)
impregnated (178)

Discussion Questions
1. Examine Ned Land's demeanor upon the *Nautilus'* arrival to the Mediterranean. *(Land insists that the time has come to escape because they are now in European territory. Land acknowledges the benefits of the voyage but believes it is time to end it, and he continues to advocate immediate escape. pp. 157–159)*

2. Discuss Aronnax's and Conseil's reactions to Land's suggestions and what this reveals about each of the three men. (*Aronnax is not ready to leave the* Nautilus *because he is completing his submarine studies and is writing a book on submarine depths. He knows he will never again have such an opportunity. Aronnax disagrees with Conseil's opinion that Nemo will release them after going over all seas of the globe and that, although they have nothing to fear from Nemo, he will not willingly release them because they know his secrets. He encourages Land to wait six months but ultimately agrees with him that they must escape if a favorable opportunity occurs. He cautions Land that a failed attempt will be disastrous because Nemo will not forgive them. pp. 157–161*)

3. Analyze what Conseil reveals about himself. (*He is disinterested in the question of escape because he has no wife, children, or relatives who expect him to return. He views himself as an extension of Aronnax, thinking and speaking like his master. He considers the choice of whether or not to try to escape as being only between Aronnax and Land. p. 159*)

4. Examine the implications of the encounter Aronnax observes between Nemo and the diver. (*A diver appears outside the submarine as Aronnax is studying the fish, and he tells Nemo. Nemo communicates and tells Aronnax the diver's name. The diver ascends, and Nemo sends a safe of gold up the iron staircase. Aronnax hears the small boat leave and return two hours later. The gold has been sent somewhere. Later, Nemo explains the source of his income and the destination of the gold. Nemo retrieves millions of dollars in gold from sunken ships. When the submarine descends to the bottom of the sea in Vigo Bay, Aronnax and Nemo watch as divers recover immeasurable treasure from a sunken French galleon. Aronnax learns that Nemo channels millions of dollars to oppressed races and individuals. pp. 162–164, 176–180*)

5. Discuss how the captives' escape plan is thwarted. (*After the* Nautilus *enters the Atlantic, Land insists the time has come to escape because they are just a few miles away from the Spanish coast. Land gives instructions to the other two for their departure at 9:00 p.m. Aronnax prepares to leave and goes about the* Nautilus *for what he presumes will be the last time. A few minutes before nine, the submarine stops on the bottom of the ocean, and Nemo appears. The submarine does not rise to the surface as it usually does. pp. 170–178*)

Supplementary Activities

1. Geography: On a map or globe, have students locate the geographical points given in this section.

2. Research: Have students research the development and opening of the Suez Canal, then pinpoint it on a map or globe as they give an oral report.

3. Literary Devices: **Similes**—"smoke was curling amongst the waves that boiled like water in a copper (p. 165) "ruins of steamers...like formidable animals" (p. 167); **Metaphor**—Atlantic: a plain incessantly ploughed by ships of all nations (p. 169)

Chapters 7–8, pp. 181–200

Nemo and Aronnax explore the ocean depths at night. Land becomes increasingly persistent about escaping. Nemo refuses to allow Land to hurt a pod of whales they encounter, but Nemo uses the *Nautilus* to massacre several cachalots that are pursuing the pod of whales.

Vocabulary
viscous (184)
effluence (184)
conflagration (184)
irradiation (186)
petrified (186)
titanic (186)
cataclysms (186)
capricious (190)
perpetual (192)
tacit (192)
carnage (198)

Discussion Questions

1. Examine details about Nemo and Aronnax's night excursion on the bottom of the sea. Brainstorm what you have heard about Atlantis, a mythical, lost continent. *(The waters are in complete darkness, but a reddish point in the distance dimly lights their way. The men walk across a vast plain with rocks and furrows as they draw closer to the light. They climb the first slopes of a mountain covered with mineralized trees and rocks. The immense number of fish and other sea creatures intrigues Aronnax. After an intense climb, the men reach the summit of the mountain, and Aronnax realizes it is a volcano. Lying beneath it are the ruins of an ancient continent Nemo identifies as Atlantis. [Note: Atlantis is a legendary continent thought to have sunk into the Atlantic due to an earthquake.] They remain at the site for an hour. Its beauty overwhelms Aronnax, and Nemo remains motionless with awe. pp. 181–188, 190–191)*

2. Discuss the reasons for Ned Land's apprehension. *(All hopes of the* Nautilus *returning to European seas vanish as the submarine remains in the midst of the Atlantic Ocean for almost three weeks, and Aronnax believes Nemo will then head into the South Pacific. With no islands in the area, escape by leaving the vessel is impossible. Land's prolonged imprisonment causes him to become increasingly silent, angry and resentful. pp. 191–194)*

3. Analyze Conseil's summation of Ned Land, beginning with "That poor Ned thinks of everything he cannot have. Everything in his past life comes back to him. Everything we are forbidden seems to him regrettable." *(Responses will vary. p. 195)*

4. Discuss the event that causes Ned to recall his days as a harpooner and the ensuing pursuit. Is Nemo fair in his response and actions? *(The* Nautilus *encounters a pod of at least twenty whales. Nemo refuses Land's request to allow the vessel to pursue the whales because it would only be for the pleasure of killing. When a troop of cachalots begins to pursue the whales, however, the captain determines to exterminate them. Using the steel spur on the prow of the* Nautilus *as a harpoon, Nemo attacks and destroys most of the cachalots, and the others flee. Land becomes enthusiastic as he watches the carnage but later says it was butchery. Nemo reminds him that they have massacred mischievous animals that would have killed the whales. pp. 195–199)*

5. **Prediction:** What will be the result of Ned Land's ill will toward Captain Nemo?

Supplementary Activities

1. Research: Have students research and bring to class information and pictures of one of the following: (a) underground volcanoes (b) the legend of the lost continent of Atlantis (c) whales and their predators. They will then participate in a class discussion.

2. Literary Devices: **Similes**—"fish rose...like birds" (p. 186) "apparatus rose like a balloon" (p. 190); **Metaphors**—ocean: Nemo's banker (p. 181) ocean: sea of blood (p. 199); **Allusion**—Homer (p. 198)

Chapters 9–10, pp. 201–214

The *Nautilus* tunnels under an ice-bank to reach the South Pole. Captain Nemo places his flag at the South Pole as the first man to set foot on that land.

Vocabulary
diorama (203)

Discussion Questions

1. Examine Aronnax's attitude and outlook concerning the possibility of Captain Nemo taking the *Nautilus* to the South Pole. Why do you think Nemo is determined to reach the Pole? *(Aronnax does not think he will do so because every prior attempt to reach the Pole has failed, and the winter season in that area is quickly approaching. He is, however, pleased at the prospect of the adventure of reaching the South Pole and finds the region remarkably beautiful. Even when the* Nautilus *is seemingly stopped by the ice-bank, Aronnax strongly desires to know what is behind it; Responses will vary. pp. 201–204)*

2. Discuss Captain Nemo's expertise in piloting the *Nautilus* as the vessel heads toward the South Pole. What dangers does he encounter? *(Nemo must pilot the submarine through treacherous, iceberg-filled waters. When submerged, ice-slips bombard the vessel from above. Nemo uses the* Nautilus *like a wedge, splitting the ice apart. When the submarine is blocked from moving, Nemo takes the* Nautilus *under the ice. He realizes the danger of not being able to renew the vessel's air supply for a few days and faces the possibility that the sea may be completely frozen over, thus preventing them from going to the surface. He takes the* Nautilus *to a depth of 400 fathoms [2400 feet]. It strikes the bottom of the ice-bank when it begins to ascend, but Nemo maneuvers the vessel until the ice-bank gradually becomes an ice-field, then surfaces to open sea. pp. 202–209)*

3. Contrast Aronnax and Land's opinion with that of Nemo as to the possibility of penetrating the ice-bank that is formed by icebergs firmly bonded together. What qualities make a strong leader? *(Land believes it is impossible to penetrate an ice-bank. Aronnax believes they are caught when solid ice forms in front of and behind the* Nautilus. *Nemo admonishes Aronnax for only seeing obstacles and difficulties with the undertaking. Nemo declares that the* Nautilus *will go all the way to the South Pole. Nemo sways Aronnax to his viewpoint. He first believes the captain will use the* Nautilus *to break up the ice. When Aronnax discovers Nemo's intent to go under the ice, he thinks Nemo can use the vessel to break through the ice to the surface; Responses will vary. pp. 204–207)*

4. Discuss hindrances to Nemo's fulfilling his dream when the *Nautilus* surfaces and the eventual outcome. How do you think Nemo would have reacted if he had failed? *(The clouds are heavy and gray, preventing Nemo from making accurate observations as to their location. On March 19, Nemo is the first person to set foot on the land, but he must have an exact instrument reading to prove he has reached the South Pole. For two days, the sun never penetrates the mists. The last possible day to obtain the reading is March 21, the day of the equinox, because the sun will then disappear below the horizon for six months. The sun appears at a quarter to twelve, March 21, allowing Nemo to make his observations. They have reached the South Pole. Nemo places his flag there and claims possession of the Pole; Responses will vary. pp. 210–214)*

5. **Prediction:** What will the *Nautilus* encounter in its attempt to reach warmer waters?

Supplementary Activities

1. Art: Have students sketch Nemo's flag as described on page 213 of the novel.

2. Research: Have students research when the South Pole was first discovered and compare their findings to the description of when Nemo stakes claim of the South Pole in the novel.

3. Creative Writing: Have students read Langston Hughes' poem, "A Dream Deferred," then model their own poem, "A Dream Achieved" based on Nemo's success.

4. Literary Devices: **Similes**—"sun's disc, like a ball of fire," "*Nautilus*, like a cetacean asleep" (p. 213); **Metaphor**—ice grouping: Oriental town (p. 202)

Chapters 11–12, pp. 215–232

The *Nautilus* becomes imprisoned in the ice, endangering the lives of the crew. The men work incessantly to chip away the ice by hand. The *Nautilus* breaks free just before the air supply is completely gone.

Vocabulary
recriminations (217)
impassive (220)
ambient (224)

Discussion Questions

1. Examine circumstances leading to a near disaster aboard the *Nautilus* and discuss whether or not it is caused by human error. *(As the* Nautilus *begins the return trip from the South Pole, those aboard experience a violent shock when a large iceberg strikes the vessel. The vessel halts, then pitches on its side, at a depth of about 180 fathoms [1080 ft.].* Nemo stops the ascension of the Nautilus *before it surfaces to prevent the possibility of being squeezed between two frozen surfaces when and if the vessel strikes against the ice-bank. When the submarine halts, it is imprisoned in a tunnel of ice about 60 feet wide. The submarine is blocked on all sides, imprisoned in the ice-bank; Responses will vary. pp. 215–223)*

2. Discuss the precarious position of the *Nautilus* and analyze the effects on the men. What character would you most likely match if you experienced such a near-disaster? Explain your choice. *(Nemo reveals anxiety, but is mostly focused on saving the* Nautilus *and her crew. Land ranges from anger to alarm. Aronnax paces anxiously, is unable to get his mind on anything else, and asks Land and Conseil to remain with him until they are out of danger. After the vessel becomes totally imprisoned, Nemo tells the captives that those aboard have two ways of dying if they cannot free the vessel. They will either be crushed to death or suffocate. The reservoir of air will be depleted in 48 hours; Responses will vary. pp. 221–224)*

3. Discuss Nemo's plans to save the *Nautilus* and the crew. *(He leads the men in an attempt to pierce 30 feet of ice by hand. He has the men make a huge trench from which to work at chipping the ice. The men work in two-hour shifts around the clock. The air in the* Nautilus *begins to fill with carbonic acid, and the lateral walls around the vessel gradually draw closer together. Realizing that the plan to chip away the ice by hand before the men die from suffocation or the walls close in is failing, Nemo begins to inject boiling water from the distilling apparatus into the water surrounding the vessel. Gradually, the water warms. When six feet of ice remain, Nemo orders the vessel to be lightened. After they fill the reservoirs with water, the vessel sinks into the hole left by the trench. Nemo then has the reservoirs filled to capacity, making the submarine heavy enough to break through the ice. Propelled by its powerful screw, the* Nautilus *breaks through the ice. pp. 221–232)*

4. Analyze the response of Nemo's crew and his captives during the struggle to survive. *(Land ceases grumbling and, along with Aronnax and Conseil, volunteers to do anything he can to help. The crew and captives work unceasingly and uncomplainingly to chip away the ice. The air becomes almost unbearable in the submarine. Conseil never leaves his master's side and expresses the desire to do without breathing in order to give Aronnax more air. When Aronnax is suffocating*

and approaching death, Conseil and Land give him the small of amount of air they find left in a diving apparatus. pp. 224–232)

Supplementary Activities

1. Creative Writing: Have students list all the emotions they have observed in the men in this section, then choose one and write a metaphor or simile that describes that emotion.

2. Research: Working in small groups, have students research submarine disasters. They are then to bring to class newspaper and magazine articles about these disasters and give an accompanying oral report.

3. Literary Devices: **Similes**—"as if our floating carriage had glided over the rails of a railroad" (p. 215) [ice] "would have crushed the sides of the *Nautilus* like glass," "seemed...that I was between the formidable jaws of a monster" (p. 227); **Metaphor**—*Nautilus*: floating carriage (p. 215)

Chapters 13–14, pp. 233–250

Ned Land's plan to escape is thwarted. Nemo, his crew, and his captives engage in a ferocious battle with giant squids. Nemo refuses Aronnax's request to set the captives free.

Vocabulary
vivifying (233)
infernal (234)
repugnant (236)
salubrious (236)
krakens (237)
vexatious (245)
nostalgia (245)

Discussion Questions

1. Examine Aronnax's response to his survival from the near-disaster of the *Nautilus* and analyze Ned Land's comment, "Your existence was worth more than ours, therefore it had to be preserved" (p. 233). Why do you think the author chooses to include this scene? *(Aronnax's first words express his gratitude to Land and Conseil because they kept him alive in the last hours before the submarine broke free to the surface. Land's comment indicates his appreciation of Aronnax's past and the possibility of future contributions to the scientific world. Land uses Aronnax's response that he is obligated to the two men and that the three of them are bound together forever to remind Aronnax of his intentions to escape and take the professor with him; Responses will vary. pp. 233–234)*

2. Discuss the importance of the direction in which the *Nautilus* proceeds from the Polar circle. *(If Nemo takes the submarine north by the Atlantic route, Aronnax will have the chance to observe more of the ocean and possibly complete the voyage around the submarine world. Because more inhabited lands are found in the Atlantic, Land will have a better chance to carry out his escape plans. The Pacific route will take them farther away from all inhabited land. pp. 234–235)*

3. Examine circumstances that thwart Land's plans to escape and discuss the feasibility of his alternate proposal. *(Nemo takes the* Nautilus *north fairly close to South America but then veers out to sea to avoid the Gulf of Mexico, thwarting Land's plan to escape to an island in the Gulf. He then proposes asking Nemo if he ever intends to grant them liberty. Aronnax believes it is useless because Nemo has avoided him since the incident at the South Pole. Aronnax thinks that Nemo will become suspicious and possibly make their lives miserable. Aronnax doesn't want to risk losing the records of his observations. pp. 235–237)*

4. Analyze the irony of the captives' conversation about the giant squid. Note Conseil's statement, "I should like to contemplate face to face one of those squids I have heard so much talk about, that can drag ships down to the bottom of the sea" (p. 237) and Land's disbelief in a monster squid. Compare the discussion of the squid to the idea of the monster the *Nautilus* was thought to be. *(Land first notices something swarming in the large seaweed close to the submarine, possibly a cavern of squids. Conseil alludes to the possibility of a monster squid, but Land says he will believe in such a monster only when he has dissected one with his own hand. Conseil refers to having seen such a monster in a picture in a church. Aronnax relates a tale of an encounter between a giant squid and a ship. Conseil begins to describe in detail the squid from Aronnax's story because he is viewing one out the window of the submarine. Conseil will get his wish to engage in combat, and Land will dismember one with his own hand; Responses will vary. pp. 237–243)*

5. Discuss the confrontation of the *Nautilus* with the squids. *(The initial squid, measuring at least 32 feet long and weighing 40,000 to 50,000 pounds, swiftly approaches the* Nautilus *and is joined by several others. The submarine suddenly stops. Nemo, looking gloomy, comes into the saloon and scrutinizes the squids, then orders the panels closed. He tells Aronnax they are going to battle the squids face-to-face because the jaws of one are caught in the branches of the submarine's screw. The battle must be fought with blades because the electric bullets are powerless against the soft flesh. Several members of the crew, the three captives, and Nemo prepare to fight the squids, and as the panels are being opened, the long arms of a squid come through the opening. Captain Nemo cuts off the tentacle, but two other tentacles snatch a sailor. Nemo rushes to the sailor's defense but is unable to rescue him. Conseil, Land, and Aronnax join in the fight, but the squid hurls out a cloud of black liquid that blinds the men, and the crewman disappears. All the men begin to fight the monsters hand-to-hand. One monster throws Ned Land down after he puts out its eyes with his harpoon and is about to cut him in two when Nemo comes to his rescue. The combat ends with the mutilated squids either dead or retreating. pp. 239–243)*

6. Examine the aftermath of the confrontation with the squids. *(Nemo, with tears rolling from his eyes, stands looking out over the sea where his companion is lost. Aronnax will forever be haunted by the cries of the dying man, whom he recognized as a Frenchman. Nemo, consumed by grief, retires to his room and allows the* Nautilus *to randomly float. The captives' escape seems possible as the vessel is relatively close to the North Carolina coast, but the bad weather prevents an attempt. Land, despondent and impatient, insists that Aronnax must speak to Nemo about their release. Even Aronnax has lost some of his enthusiasm about the voyage. pp. 244–246)*

7. Discuss the confrontation between Aronnax and Nemo and its consequences. *(After receiving no response to his knock, Aronnax enters Nemo's room and finds him bent over his worktable. He is working on a manuscript of his studies of the sea, which he will enclose in an unsinkable case to be thrown into the sea by the last survivor aboard the* Nautilus. *Aronnax offers to preserve Nemo's manuscript if he will give the captives their liberty. Nemo responds with the same answer of seven months before, whoever enters his vessel never leaves it again. Nemo says they will never again discuss the matter. When Aronnax reports his conversation to Land, he insists they will escape as the* Nautilus *approaches Long Island, regardless of the weather. Symptoms of a hurricane make their escape impossible. pp. 246–250)*

8. **Prediction:** How will the voyage end? Explain your response.

Supplementary Activities

1. Art/Creative Writing: Have students sketch the giant squid or write Nemo's journal entry after the fight with the squids.

2. Drama: Working in small groups, have students stage one of the following scenes: (a) the interaction of the three captives after their escape from the ice-bank (b) the conversation between Land and Aronnax about asking Nemo to release them (c) the confrontation between Nemo and Aronnax about the captives' release.

3. Literary Devices: **Similes**—"arms glided like a serpent" (p. 241); **Metaphor**—squids: vermin (p. 241)

Chapters 15–17, pp. 251–272

Nemo and his men attack and annihilate a ship and its crew. Just as the captives prepare to escape by boat, the *Nautilus* is dragged into a maëlstrom. The captives' boat breaks free, and the men land safely on an island. The fate of the *Nautilus* and its crew is unknown.

Vocabulary
hecatomb (251)
proximity (251)
pendant (254)
coalesced (256)
salient (260)
inundated (261)
hyperborean (264)
poignant (266)
maëlstrom (269)

Discussion Questions

1. Discuss the significance of the discovery of the sunken ship, the *Vengeur* and its effect on Captain Nemo. *(Nemo relates the story of the* Vengeur, *which had been sunk 74 years before, after a heroic fight. All 356 sailors aboard refused to surrender, and all perished. Nemo's display of emotion causes Aronnax to realize it is extreme hatred and a desire for vengeance, not a dislike or distrust of people in general, that causes Nemo to live as a man without a country. pp. 252–255)*

2. Examine circumstances and results of the confrontation between the *Nautilus* and the warship. *(After the* Nautilus *surfaces, the warship, whose country Nemo recognizes but does not share, begins to pursue the vessel. As the ship draws near, the captives foresee a chance to escape, but the warship fires at the* Nautilus. *Conseil believes the ship's crew think they have sighted the narwhal that attacked the* Abraham Lincoln. *Aronnax realizes the warship is pursuing with the intent to destroy the* Nautilus *because Captain Farragut had discovered and spread the word that the "narwhal" is actually a submarine. He believes Nemo uses the submarine as an instrument of vengeance. When Land attempts to wave his handkerchief in the air to signal the warship, Nemo knocks it from his hand. He screams at the warship, orders the captives below, and announces his intention to sink the ship. Members of Nemo's crew display the same hatred. The captives go below. Aronnax disagrees with Nemo's intense hatred which makes it better for the captives to try to escape and perish rather than be accomplices in Nemo's retaliation. Nemo's crew prepares for battle and, just before the captives jump into the water, the* Nautilus *begins to submerge. Nemo plans to attack the warship from below, propelling his vessel through the other ship's hull. All aboard perish as the warship sinks. pp. 254–262)*

3. Analyze what Nemo's reaction to the warship reveals about him. *(Hatred consumes him. He is determined to destroy the warship and its crew at the spot the* Vengeur *lies beneath the ocean. He believes that he represents justice and that he is the oppressed and the warship the oppressor. He reveals that his hatred centers on his belief that the country from which the warship comes caused him to lose all he loved, i.e., his country, wife, children, and parents. After the warship sinks, Nemo*

kneels, weeping, before a portrait of a young woman and two little children. Aronnax does not sympathize with Nemo and begins to believe that escaping is the only option. pp. 257–258)

4. Discuss the captives' plans following the destruction of the warship and the ensuing events. *(After the submarine keeps a northerly course for several days, Land sights land about twenty miles away and makes preparations for the trio to escape. They are to meet at the boat at 10:00 p.m. Aronnax spends the remaining hours reflecting on his adventures aboard the* Nautilus. *Just before Land releases the boat, they hear a cry, "The Maëlstrom!" [p. 269] and realize the submarine is being dragged into a dangerous whirlpool. The small boat in which the three men remain breaks loose from the submarine as it is being tossed about. The men escape and land on an island. pp. 263–271)*

5. What do you think about Nemo's final words? *(Responses will vary. Suggestion: As Aronnax is preparing to escape, Nemo comes toward him but does not see him. He is sobbing, "Almighty God! Enough! Enough!" Aronnax later questions whether or not Nemo deliberately steered his submarine into the maëlstrom. pp. 268–269)*

6. Examine Aronnax's thoughts after his escape. *(He believes it is unfeasible for he and his companions to return to France right away because they have no way to report their location. They must wait for the routine arrival of a steamer. He recalls and records all the facts about his adventures. He understands that others may not believe that he has spent ten months under the seas and has traveled 20,000 leagues exploring the marvels of the world's oceans and seas. He speculates on whether or not Nemo and the* Nautilus *survived. He hopes the submarine and its captain conquered the maëlstrom and that Nemo's hatred is now appeased. pp. 271–272)*

Supplementary Activities

1. Creative Writing: Have students explain in a short paragraph what they think happened to Nemo, beginning with, "I believe Captain Nemo..."

2. Research: Have students research and prepare an oral report about the maëlstrom current in the Arctic Ocean, including information about ships that have been lost in the whirlpool.

3. Art: Have students sketch their impression of the battle between the *Nautilus* and the warship, based on the following metaphors: *Nautilus:* engine of destruction (p. 255); *Nautilus:* steel-plated cigar; water: liquid bed (p. 260); sinking ship: human ant-hill (p. 261).

4. Literary Devices: **Similes**—"pendant, which streamed like a narrow ribbon" (p. 254); [boat] "sprang like a stone from a sling" (p. 270); **Metaphor**—chords of the organ: wails of a soul (p. 267)

Post-reading Discussion Questions

1. Use the Character Web on page 6 of this guide to discuss both Captain Nemo and Professor Aronnax. *(Students' responses will vary. Suggestions: Aronnax's statements reflect his amazement over the wonders of the Nautilus and underwater sights. He acts courteously and civilly. He fears what Captain Nemo's wrath may lead to and for his life at the South Pole. He thinks he wants to stay aboard the Nautilus long enough to learn all he can about submarine life. He looks intelligent and refined. Others treat him with respect. Captain Nemo's statements reflect his bitterness and vindictiveness. He acts arrogantly at times but also shows grief and compassion. He thinks he will never allow the captives to leave. He looks powerful and vigorous. Others treat him with obedience and, at times, fear.)*

2. Using the Character Chart on page 9 of this guide, discuss episodes in the book in which each of the men experiences various emotions. *(Students' responses will vary.)*

3. Use the Story Map on page 10 of this guide to discuss the plot of the novel. *(Setting: oceans and seas of the world, 1866–1867; Characters: Professor Aronnax, Captain Nemo, Conseil, Ned Land; Problem: Captain Nemo takes the other three men captive aboard his submarine, where they learn of his desire for vengeance against humanity; Conflict: [1] Captain Nemo informs the captives that he will never allow them to leave his vessel. [2] The Nautilus must battle giant squids. [3] The Nautilus engages in conflict with a warship. Climax: The submarine is caught in a maëlstrom; Turning point: The captives are in a small boat that breaks loose from the Nautilus; Resolution: Aronnax, Conseil, and Land survive; the fate of Captain Nemo and his vessel is unknown.)*

4. Complete the Story Map on page 11 of this guide. Select the five events from the story you think are most important, then list them in the blocks. *(Students' responses will vary.)*

5. Using the Thematic Analysis graphic organizer on page 12 of this guide, select a theme from the book and brainstorm how the theme is developed in the book. *(Students' responses will vary. Suggestions: Loyalty: Conseil to Aronnax; Captain Nemo's crew to him; Captain Nemo to his crew; Conseil and Land's willingness to give Aronnax the little air that is left; Land will not attempt to leave without the others; Captain Nemo's burial of his crewman; Captain Nemo's grief when another crewman dies.)*

6. Discuss the effectiveness of Aronnax as the first-person narrator and how the story might have changed if Captain Nemo had been the narrator. *(Students' responses will vary.)*

7. Analyze Captain Nemo: (a) what country he comes from (b) possible causes for his bitterness (c) what country the warship is from and why he is determined to destroy it (d) the identity of the woman and children in the portrait and what happened to them (e) whether or not he survived. *(Students' responses will vary.)*

8. Analyze why Conseil is so loyal to Aronnax. Speculate on what happened in the past. *(Students' responses will vary.)*

9. Place the following values in a vertical line on an overhead transparency: Accomplishments, Loyalty, Wealth, Skill, Self-respect, Respect for others, Honesty, Impartiality, Wealth, Kindness. Place the names Captain Nemo and Professor Aronnax in columns across the top. Brainstorm with students and rank the importance of the values for each character, with #1 being the highest.

10. Analyze the resolution of the novel. Discuss whether or not Captain Nemo survived, what will happen to Aronnax and the others when they return to their own countries, and whether or not Aronnax and Captain Nemo will ever meet again.

Post-reading Extension Activities

Note: Starred activities indicate enrichment for accelerated students.

Writing

1. Write name poems for two of the characters.

2. Write a newspaper article about the return of Professor Aronnax to France.

3. Write a cinquain poem about one of the themes in the book. Pattern—Line 1: one word (noun) to give the title; Line 2: two words to describe the title; Line 3: three words to express action concerning the title; Line 4: four words to express feeling about the title; Line 5: one word that is a synonym for the title.

4. *Using the Venn diagram (see page 13 of this guide) for planning, write an essay comparing and contrasting Captain Nemo and Professor Aronnax.

5. Write an epilogue for the novel, including what happens to Captain Nemo and his crew.

Art

1. Create a montage of pictures portraying the geographical points of the journey.

2. Draw a sketch of the *Nautilus*.

3. Prepare a poster to advertise the book.

4. *Create a plaster of Paris or papier-mâché model of the *Nautilus*.

Current Events

1. Bring to class newspaper or magazine articles about submarine disasters.

2. *Prepare an oral report tracing the history of the United States' first nuclear submarine, the *Nautilus*.

Viewing

View a movie version of *Twenty Thousand Leagues Under the Sea* and present an oral comparison of the movie with the novel.

Listening/Speaking

Play appropriate background music as you read a selection from the book to the class.

Additional Reading

*Read *A Man Without a Country* by Edward Everett Hale. Using the Venn diagram (see page 13 of this guide) for planning, write an essay comparing and contrasting the lives of Philip Nolan and Captain Nemo.

Assessment for *Twenty Thousand Leagues Under the Sea*

Assessment is an ongoing process. The following ten items can be completed during the novel study. Once finished, the student and teacher will check the work. Points may be added to indicate the level of understanding.

Name _____ Date _____

Student	Teacher	
_____	_____	1. Write three questions you would like to ask Professor Aronnax about the journey. Exchange with a partner and answer his or her questions.
_____	_____	2. Write a riddle about one of the characters in the book. Read your riddle aloud to the class and have them guess the name of the character.
_____	_____	3. Correct any quizzes you have taken over the novel.
_____	_____	4. Display your extension project on the assigned day. Be prepared to explain your project.
_____	_____	5. Participate in a vocabulary "bee." You are to supply the definition of each word rather than the spelling.
_____	_____	6. Compare any activities, such as Character Charts and Story Maps, in small groups of three or four.
_____	_____	7. Working in a small group, prepare and present a press conference for Professor Aronnax after he returns to France.
_____	_____	8. Working with a partner, present one of the scenes from the novel in charades and have the class guess the scene you are portraying.
_____	_____	9. Write a review about the book for the school newspaper. Use at least ten of your vocabulary words from the novel.
_____	_____	10. Participate in a class discussion about the types of conflict Captain Nemo faced. Provide examples from the novel.

Glossary

Part One, Pages 9–28
inexplicable (9): cannot be explained, understood, or accounted for; mysterious
impunity (11): freedom from harm
prodigious (12): huge, immense
formidable (12): difficult to overcome or defeat; powerful
enigma (14): baffling or puzzling person, problem, or situation
veritable (18): true, real, actual
savants (18): scholars; men of learning

Pages 29–52
malediction (34): speaking evil of or to a person; curse
indefatigably (34): persistently
abyss (36): bottomless pit; lowest depth
imperturbable (37): not easily excited or disturbed; calm
vertiginous (40): whirling, revolving, spinning around
infamous (46): shameful; wicked; having a bad reputation
implacable (52): difficult to soothe

Pages 53–79
despots (58): leaders with absolute power
vivacity (73): liveliness, animation, pep

Pages 80–101
ironical (81): expressing one thing and meaning the opposite
contiguous (82): adjoining; very close together
voracious (89): greedy
Protestant (95): a member of a Christian church not governed by the Roman Catholic Church or
    the Eastern Church
complaisant (99): willing to do what is asked; eager to please

Pages 102–115
circumspection (105): watchful and cautious observation
middling (106): ordinary, average; medium in size or quality
ecstasy (109): great joy; rapture
pirogues (111): canoes hollowed from the trunks of trees
equilibrium (111): balance, stability
frigate (112): fast, medium-sized warship with three masts
vociferations (114): noisy speeches; clamorous, agitated outcries
gambols (114): acts of running and jumping about; frolics

Pages 116–128
interdicted (118): prohibited or forbidden
imperious (118): haughty, arrogant, domineering
soporific (120): characterized by deep, unnatural sleep; hypnotic
morbid (120): abnormal, horrible, gruesome
physiognomy (122): a person's face; countenance
spasmodic (123): brief, irregular, intermittent
inextricable (125): that which cannot be disentangled; confusing, jumbled

Part Two, Pages 131–155
disdain (131): to look down on or consider beneath oneself; contempt, arrogance
crypt (143): underground room or vault
foliated (144): having thin, leaf-like layers
limpidity (144): clearness, distinctness, clarity

opaque (147): not letting light through; not transparent
audacious (147): having courage to take risks; bold, daring
labyrinth (150): a number of connecting passages arranged in a difficult pattern; maze
ulterior (152): intentionally concealed or kept in the background; hidden
epoch (152): a period of time; era
subterranean (153): beneath the earth's surface; underground

Pages 156–180
annihilate (159): to completely destroy
hermetically (161): sealed so that no air can escape
taciturn (161): unusually silent and uncommunicative
infinite (173): endless
mortal (175): very great, deadly, dire
impregnated (178): filled, saturated

Pages 181–200
viscous (184): thick and sticky, like heavy syrup
effluence (184): an outward flow of water, light, electricity, or magnetism
conflagration (184): big, destructive fire
irradiation (186): ray of light; illumination
petrified (186): turned into stone
titanic (186): having great size, strength, or power; huge, gigantic
cataclysms (186): sudden, violent changes in the earth; e.g., floods or earthquakes
capricious (190): changeable; likely to change suddenly
perpetual (192): lasting forever; eternal
tacit (192): implied or understood without being openly expressed
carnage (198): slaughter of a great number of people or animals; massacre

Pages 201–214
diorama (203): scene or exhibit showing lifelike; sculpted figures against a painted or molded background

Pages 215–232
recriminations (217): acts of accusing in retaliation; counter accusations
impassive (220): without feeling or emotion; unmoved
ambient (224): all around; circulating

Pages 233–250
vivifying (233): outrageous, detestable, abominable
infernal (234): fit to have come from hell; outrageous, detestable
repugnant (236): disagreeable or offensive
salubrious (236): favorable to good health; wholesome
krakens (237): mythical sea monsters of enormous size
vexatious (245): annoying, bothersome
nostalgia (245): painful, wistful yearning for persons, places, or things of the past

Pages 251–272
hecatomb (251): a great slaughter; sacrifice
proximity (251): nearness, adjacency
pendant (254): flag, banner
coalesced (256): merged, consolidated, united
salient (260): standing out; prominent, easily noticed
inundated (261): overflowed, overwhelmed
hyperborean (264): of the far north; arctic, frigid
poignant (266): distressing to the mind
maëlstrom (269): great or turbulent whirlpool